P9-CRM-812

the pumpkin cookbook

hamlyn

the pumpkin cookbook

Notes

1 The American Egg Board advises that eggs should not be consumed raw. This book contains some dishes made with raw or lightly cooked eggs. It is prudent for more vulnerable people such as pregnant and nursing mothers, invalids, the elderly, babies, and young children to avoid uncooked or lightly cooked dishes made with eggs.

2 Meat and poultry should be cooked thoroughly. To test if poultry is cooked, pierce the flesh through the thickest part with a skewer or fork – the juices should run clear, never pink or red. Keep refrigerated until ready for cooking.

3 This book includes dishes made with nuts and nut derivatives. It is advisable for those with known allergic reactions to nuts and nut derivatives and those who may potentially be vulnerable to these allergies, such as pregnant and nursing mothers, invalids, the elderly, babies, and children, to avoid dishes made with nuts and nut oils. It is also prudent to check the labels of pre-prepared ingredients for the possible inclusion of nut derivatives.

First published in 2001
by Hamlyn
a division of Octopus Publishing Group Limited
2–4 Heron Quays, London, E14 4JP

ISBN 0 600 60383 0

Printed and bound in China

10 9 8 7 6 5 4 3 2

Photographer: Philip Webb
Food Stylist: David Morgan
Front Jacket Photographer: Graham Kirk
Front Jacket Food Stylist: Joanna Farrow

Contents

Introduction 6

Appetizers and Side Dishes 12

Main Courses 20

Sweets, Breads, and Accompaniments 36

Index 64

introduction

Pumpkins are among the few truly seasonal vegetables left, and the arrival of these glorious golden vegetables marks the start of the fall season and fills most of us with a nostalgic longing for Halloween and Thanksgiving. Pumpkins can be stored in a cool, dry place for several months, but they will rarely survive in good condition until spring, so it's important to make the most of them when they are around.

Despite their strong connections with Halloween and Thanksgiving, pumpkins are also wonderful culinary ingredients in their own right and there's no reason to wait for the holidays to make use of them. They are among the most versatile of vegetables lending themselves to just about any part of a meal. The best pumpkins for cooking are the sugar pumpkin which has sweet flesh and is recommended for pies and baking, and the turban pumpkin which comes in a variety of shapes, sizes and colors, all characterized by a Turkish topknot. The delicious, nutritious flesh of these pumpkins can be turned into warming soups, salads, casseroles, stir-fries, or vegetable accompaniments, and can even be used to create a range of tempting hot and cold desserts. This book will show you just how versatile the pumpkin can be, with a mouthwatering selection of imaginative recipes for all occasions.

Facts and Figures

Pumpkins are members of the *Cucurbita*, or gourd, family, which also includes melons, cucumbers, summer squashes, and winter squashes. The names are often used interchangeably, but a pumpkin is usually understood to be a large, orange, winter squash with a hard skin and rich orange flesh. Sizes vary hugely, from miniature varieties to prize-winning giants of over 900 pounds. In fact, many varieties, including Atlantic Giant and Big Max, are bred for size, and there are pumpkin contests held all over the country during the fall months. The record so far is 990 pounds but the contests continue. Other varieties, including Munchkin, are bred to be miniatures, and these make charming decorations for Halloween.

Pumpkins have been cultivated for many thousands of years in various countries around the world. In this country, native Americans taught the early settlers to grow a variety of squashes, which the settlers called pumpion (perhaps from the Greek word for melon, *pepon*). The settlers also adopted the Narragansett word *askutasquash*, which they changed to squash. They soon realized just how valuable these vegetables were and we have been growing a wide selection ever since. Pumpkins are easy to grow and the delicious flesh is packed with nutrients, making them a reliable and indispensable crop.

Fresh pumpkin has high levels of vitamin A, potassium, phosphorus, iron, calcium, and magnesium. A cup of mashed pumpkin flesh only contains about 85 calories. The seeds are also high in phosphorus and potassium, and provide protein, iron, zinc, and vitamin A, so not only does it taste delicious, it is also very good for you too.

Growing Pumpkins

There is an old saying: "To be a successful gardener, grow pumpkins." And that is how easy they are to grow. The only problem you may encounter is choosing which type of pumpkin to grow as there are hundreds of varieties, each with its own characteristics.

If you are growing pumpkins for carving into traditional jack-o-lanterns, plant the Connecticut Field Pumpkin, with its classic shape and orange color. Like all pumpkins, these are also edible, so you can turn the discarded flesh into a delicious pie or casserole. However, if you intend to grow pumpkins solely for eating, choose a variety that has been bred specially for this purpose because it will have a more intense flavor.

If you have trouble deciding, why not try growing more than one variety? They will grow together in the same patch and you'll get a good selection. You can also compare the vegetables you harvest from your plants to help you decide what to plant next year.

All pumpkins grow on long vines with large hairy leaves. The plants can take up quite a lot of space, but the vines can be encouraged to grow in the direction you choose, and can even be trained over a shed roof to save space.

Pumpkin plants love a sunny spot, the sunnier the better. Sow the seeds in the spring when the temperature consistently reaches the low 70s. In colder climates, the seeds can be started off indoors in small pots and the growing plants can be moved outside when the weather has warmed up.

For best results, sow the seeds in the middle of a mound of earth about three feet across, surrounded by a shallow moat to hold water around the roots. Add a little nutrient-rich compost or aged manure to give them a helping hand. You can sow up to six seeds in each mound, then cover them with about an inch of soil. Keep the soil moist and the pumpkin plants will soon appear. When they are two weeks old, thin out the smaller plants, leaving just the two or three strongest ones, and discard the others. Let them grow, watering them when the soil dries. You will be rewarded with a fruitful harvest.

Halloween

Halloween is the time for trick-or-treating, for dressing up, and for scary-faced jack-o-lanterns. Pumpkins have been a symbol of Halloween for many generations and this holiday is characterized by a huge array of pumpkins of all shapes and sizes appearing all over the country. But how did the festival originate?

The story begins with the Celts who lived in the United Kingdom and northern France around two thousand years ago. To them, October 31 was the last day of the old year, when the warmth of summer was over and the bleakness of winter was upon them. At this time of year it seemed that the world was dying, so they honored their god of death, Samhain. The Celts believed that Samhain allowed the souls of dead ancestors to return to earth on this night.

Each family extinguished their hearth fire to symbolize the dying of the world. The Celts' religious leaders, the Druids, lit sacred bonfires and festivals were held around them. When the festivities were over, each family lit a torch from the sacred bonfire and took it home to relight their hearth fire and symbolize the beginning of the new year. The torches were also believed to scare away evil spirits with their sacred flames, and to light the way for the souls of the dead ancestors as they walked the earth.

As Christianity spread through the region, many of the old Celtic customs were combined with Christian festivals. The festival of All Saints' Day, or All Hallows' Day as it was also known, fell on November 1, so the Celtic customs associated with Samhain were combined with it and it became known as All Hallows' Eve, and eventually Halloween.

Jack-o-lanterns

The Halloween custom of carving jack-o-lanterns is thought to have come from Ireland. Irish folklore tells of a man named Jack, a notorious joker and trickster, who tricked the devil into climbing up a tree. While the devil was up in the tree, Jack carved a cross in the tree's bark, trapping the devil in the branches above. Jack then made a deal with the devil that he would let him out of the tree only if the devil promised not to tempt him again.

According to the tale, after Jack died he was denied a place in Heaven because of his evil ways. However, he was also denied a place in Hell because he had tricked the devil. Instead the devil gave him a single ember, placed in a hollowed-out turnip to keep it burning, with which to light his way through the darkness. Like all the other dead souls, Jack returned to walk the earth on October 31 and could be seen using his lantern to light the way.

When Irish immigrants came to America, they carved the more readily available pumpkins rather than turnips to hold the flame, and candles rather than embers to light their Jack's Lanterns.

Pumpkin carving has a place in everyone's heart, whatever their age. Whether it is a frightened ghost, a scary monster, a Halloween cat, or any other face, a carved pumpkin can be a way to exercise your creativity. Start by cutting the top off the pumpkin, angling the knife outward so that the lid is wider than the base. Scoop out the seeds and fibers and save the seeds for toasting. Next, use a strong spoon to scoop out some of the pumpkin flesh to make the walls thinner and easier to carve.

For a simple design, draw the face straight onto the pumpkin with a fine permanent marker, then cut out the shapes with a sharp knife, taking care to remove all traces of pen lines. If you are planning a more complicated design, draw it on paper first, to make sure you get it right, then lay the paper over the pumpkin. Pleat the paper as necessary so that it sits smoothly over the surface, then transfer the design to the pumpkin by making small holes through the paper into the skin using a toothpick or small skewer. Make the holes close enough together so that when you remove the paper, the features appear as smooth lines of holes on the pumpkin skin. Use a sharp knife to carve out the features, carefully following the marked lines. Alternatively for a different design use the stem of the pumpkin to represent the nose and cut out the eyes and the nose around this. The cut off pumpkin top can be used to make a hat.

When the jack-o-lantern is ready, place a short, wide candle in the bottom, light it and replace the pumpkin lid. Then turn out the lights and admire your handiwork.

Pumpkin carving is great fun, but it's safer for small children to simply draw their scary faces on miniature pumpkins using permanent markers. These make fabulous Halloween decorations and there is no danger of cuts and scrapes.

Thanksgiving

The traditional feast of roast turkey, cranberries, corn, and pumpkin pie has been with us for generations. This much-loved national holiday originated in the fall of 1621 when Plymouth governor William Bradford wanted to give thanks for the bountiful harvest the pilgrims had that year. The governor invited the neighboring native Americans to join the pilgrims for a three-day feast and holiday. By the end of the 19th century, Thanksgiving Day had become a tradition in New England and was finally proclaimed a national holiday in 1863 by Abraham Lincoln.

Since then, this traditional feast has become part of American culture. Traditionally celebrated on the last Thursday in November, Thanksgiving was moved to the fourth Thursday of the month by an act of Congress in 1941. Canada first adopted Thanksgiving in 1879 and now celebrates it on the second Monday in October. For most Americans and Canadians, Thanksgiving just wouldn't be Thanksgiving without the humble pumpkin.

Cooking with Pumpkin

Despite the strong holiday associations, you don't have to wait for Thanksgiving to eat pumpkin, and you don't need the excuse of having the appealing leftover pulp from your Halloween jack-o-lantern to try one of the wonderful recipes in this book. Buy a beautiful, fresh pumpkin whenever you can and try out different ways to cook it, to discover just how versatile and flavorful it can be.

Choose pumpkins that are heavy for their size and clean and bright in appearance, without any cracks or bruises. They should sound hollow when you tap them. If you are buying pre-cut pumpkin, in wedges or slices, check that the flesh looks moist and make sure that it is well wrapped, so that it does not dry out. Uncut pumpkins can be stored in a cool, dry place for several months, but once they have been cut open, the exposed surface must be covered , they can be kept in the refrigerator for up to 2 weeks.

To peel a pumpkin, first slice it in half from top to bottom then cut it into wedges like a melon and remove the seeds and fibres. You can then remove the skin with a very sharp knife

If you have any leftovers, you can freeze portions of cooked, mashed pumpkin and eat them when fresh pumpkins are out of season. Alternatively, use canned pumpkin which makes a great pantry standby. A 16-ounce can of pumpkin purée is equivalent to around two cups of fresh pumpkin. However, use fresh pumpkin when you can, as it is much healthier with many more vitamins, and the texture is better, too.

Even the seeds of a pumpkin can be turned into a delicious snack. First preheat the oven to 325–350°F. Remove the pumpkin flesh and fibers from around the seeds and rinse them well. Spread them in a single layer on an ungreased cookie sheet. Bake in the preheated oven for 15–30 minutes, or until the seeds are dry and golden. The longer you leave them, the crispier they will become. Toasted pumpkin seeds make a great snack for children and are very nutritious, too. Add salt if you like and serve a bowl of them with drinks, before a meal, or just dip in whenever you feel like a snack. Alternatively try the recipe for Caramelized Pumpkin Seeds on page 62.

tuscan pumpkin soup

1 pumpkin, about 4 pounds

4 tablespoons olive oil

2 tablespoons butter

1 onion, roughly chopped

2 large garlic cloves, roughly chopped

2 starchy potatoes, roughly chopped

4 cups chicken stock

¼ teaspoon ground cinnamon

½ cup heavy cream

salt and pepper

light cream and pumpkin crisps, to serve

1 Cut the pumpkin into quarters or eighths. Scoop out the seeds and fibers, then peel the pumpkin pieces and roughly chop the flesh.

2 Heat the oil and butter in a large, heavy-based saucepan until it is foaming. Add the onion and cook gently, stirring frequently, for about 5 minutes until it is softened but not colored. Add the chopped pumpkin, garlic, and potatoes, and cook gently, stirring frequently, for a further 5 minutes.

3 Pour in the stock, add the cinnamon, season with salt and pepper to taste and bring to a boil. Half-cover the pan and simmer gently for 30 minutes or until the vegetables are soft.

4 Pour the soup in batches into a food processor and process until smooth, then return to the pan. Add the cream and reheat, stirring frequently, then add water to thin slightly if necessary. Taste for seasoning.

5 Pour the soup into warmed bowls, drizzle with light cream, and grind black pepper over the top. Serve immediately topped with some pumpkin crisps.

Serves 4–6
Preparation time: 20 minutes
Cooking time: 30 minutes

pumpkin crisps

1 small pumpkin

vegetable oil, for deep-frying

salt

1 Slice the pumpkin flesh into fine wafers using a potato peeler or mandoline.

2 Heat 2 inches of vegetable oil in a heavy-based pan until very hot. Pat dry the pumpkin wafers.

3 Deep-fry the wafers in batches for 30 seconds, or until crisp and golden. Serve seasoned with salt, or use as a garnish.

Serves 4–6
Preparation time: 5 minutes
Cooking time: 5 minutes

pumpkin soup with crusty cheese topping

1½ tablespoons sunflower or olive oil

1 large onion, finely chopped

3 garlic cloves, crushed

2 celery sticks, chopped

1½ pounds pumpkin flesh, roughly chopped

3 cups vegetable or chicken stock

pinch of grated nutmeg

1 bay leaf

a few parsley stalks

⅓ cup light cream or half-and-half

1–2 tablespoons finely chopped parsley, plus extra to garnish

salt and pepper

To garnish:

1 small baguette

½ cup grated Gruyère cheese

½ cup light cream or crème fraîche (optional)

1 Heat the oil in a saucepan and fry the onion and garlic until soft but not brown. Add the celery and pumpkin flesh and fry for 10–15 minutes to draw out the flavors. Stir in the stock and nutmeg. Tie the bay leaf and parsley stalks together with string, add to the saucepan, and bring to a boil. Reduce the heat and simmer for about 30 minutes until the vegetables are soft.

2 Remove the bouquet of herbs and purée the soup in a food processor or blender. Alternatively, pass it through a fine sieve. Return the purée to the saucepan, bring to a boil and season with salt and pepper. Stir in the cream and chopped parsley, return to a boil, then reduce the heat and keep the soup warm while preparing the garnish.

3 Cut the baguette into 8 slices, place them on a baking sheet and toast under a preheated broiler until pale golden on both sides. Leave the broiler on.

4 Pour the hot soup into 4 deep ovenproof bowls. Arrange 2 pieces of the baguette in each one, overlapping them slightly. Sprinkle the bread with grated cheese. Place the bowls on the baking sheet and broil until the cheese is golden brown and bubbling. Garnish with parsley and a small swirl of light cream or crème fraîche, if liked. Serve immediately.

Serves 4
Preparation time: 25 minutes
Cooking time: 1¼ hours

curried pumpkin and sweet onions

4–5 tablespoons vegetable oil

3 large onions, chopped

1 garlic clove, crushed

2 teaspoons garam masala

⅓ teaspoon ground cloves

1 pumpkin, about 1½ pounds, peeled and roughly chopped

2 red chiles, finely chopped

1 x 8-ounce can chopped tomatoes

1 cup water

2 teaspoons dark brown sugar

1 tablespoon white wine vinegar

salt and pepper

In southern Goa, in India, they cook pumpkin in this delicious sweet but chile-hot curry. As with all Goan cooking, vinegar is added once the curry has reduced to a thick sauce. Serve with chicken or fish curry and a rice dish. Garam masala is a spice mix that can be found in Indian markets and gourmet stores.

1 Heat the oil in a large saucepan and fry the onions for 20 minutes or until golden brown and caramelized.

2 Add the garlic, garam masala, and ground cloves to the onions and cook for 1 minute, stirring constantly.

3 Add the chopped pumpkin to the pan and toss in the oil for a couple of minutes, until it is beginning to brown. Add the chopped chiles, tomatoes, water, and brown sugar, cover and simmer gently for 25–30 minutes or until the pumpkin is very tender.

4 Add the vinegar, season to taste with salt and pepper and serve immediately.

Serves 4
Preparation time: 10 minutes
Cooking time: about 1 hour

roasted pumpkin wedges

1 pumpkin, about 3 pounds

4 tablespoons extra virgin olive oil

several sprigs of thyme

2 tablespoons pumpkin seeds

salt and pepper

To serve:

crème fraîche

cilantro leaves

Serve this dish as a vegetable accompaniment to grilled or roasted meats. If you like, try other herbs such as rosemary or sage instead of the thyme sprigs.

1 Scoop out the seeds and fibers from the pumpkin. Cut the pumpkin into thick wedges and place them skin sides down in a roasting pan.

2 Drizzle the wedges with the olive oil, scatter with the thyme and pumpkin seeds and season with salt and pepper. Bake in a preheated oven at 425°F for 40–45 minutes until tender and roasted.

3 Transfer to serving plates, spoon over a little crème fraîche and scatter with cilantro leaves.

Serves 4
Preparation time: 5 minutes
Cooking time: 40–45 minutes

grilled pumpkin with parmesan

1 pumpkin (about 2 pounds), seeded and cut into small wedges or slices

⅓ cup butter

5 ounces Parmesan cheese

sea salt flakes and pepper

1 Heat a grill pan, add the pumpkin in batches, and cook for about 10 minutes on each side. As the pumpkin wedges are cooked, put them on a large plate and keep warm.

2 Melt the butter in a small pan and heat until it just begins to brown, to give it a rich, nutty flavor. Pour the butter over the cooked pumpkin and season with salt and pepper. Using a vegetable peeler, shave the Parmesan directly onto the pumpkin and serve immediately, or slightly warm (while the butter is still melted).

Serves 4
Preparation time: 10 minutes
Cooking time: 40 minutes

pumpkin, pine nut, and oregano salad

1 small pumpkin, about 1 pound, halved, seeded, and cut into 1-inch wedges

6 ounces fresh corn kernels, removed from the cob

2 yellow zucchini, cut diagonally into ½-inch pieces

½ cup toasted pine nuts

small bunch of oregano, chopped

5 tablespoons lemon-infused olive oil

sea salt flakes and pepper

Lemon-infused oil is available in delicatessens and gourmet food stores. You will find it easier to drizzle the olive oil if you have a pouring stopper — the oil should flow in a fine stream so that it is evenly dispersed.

1 Heat a grill pan, add the pumpkin in batches and cook on all sides until soft, about 6 minutes on each side. To test, insert the tip of a knife into the thickest part of the pumpkin, it should go in easily. Arrange the pumpkin on a large serving dish.

2 Add the corn to the grill pan and cook for 6 minutes, moving them constantly until they are lightly charred. Arrange on the same dish as the pumpkin. Add the zucchini pieces and cook for 2 minutes on each side, then add to the other vegetables.

3 Sprinkle the pine nuts, chopped oregano, and salt and pepper over the salad and drizzle with the lemon oil. Serve immediately.

Serves 4
Preparation time: 20 minutes
Cooking time: about 40 minutes

pumpkin and couscous pilaf

1¼ cups couscous

¾ cup water

½ teaspoon saffron threads

1 cup vegetable stock

5 tablespoons olive oil

1 onion, finely chopped

¾ pound fresh pumpkin flesh, diced

long strip of lemon zest

1 cinnamon stick

2 bay leaves

1 cup flaked almonds

salt and pepper

mint or dill sprigs, to garnish

1 Put the couscous into a bowl. Pour the water over it and leave to soak for 15 minutes. Add the saffron to the stock and set it aside to infuse.

2 Heat 3½ tablespoons of the oil in a saucepan. Add the onion and fry until translucent, then add the pumpkin and fry until the onion and pumpkin are lightly colored.

3 Drain the couscous and add to the pan with the saffron liquid, lemon rind, cinnamon, bay leaves, and salt and pepper. Bring to a boil, then simmer very gently, uncovered, until most of the liquid has evaporated.

4 Meanwhile, heat the remaining oil in a heavy-based frying pan, add the almonds and cook, stirring frequently, until evenly browned.

5 Remove the cinnamon, bay leaves, and lemon rind from the pilaf, if desired, then gently stir in the almonds. Garnish with mint or dill and serve.

Serves 4
Preparation time: 10 minutes
Cooking time: 20 minutes

pumpkin, sage, and chile risotto

½ cup butter

1 large onion, finely chopped

1–2 fresh or dried red chiles, seeded, and finely chopped

1 pumpkin, about 1 pound, peeled and roughly chopped

2¼ cups Arborio or Vialone Nano rice

5 cups hot chicken or vegetable stock

3 tablespoons chopped sage

1 cup grated Parmesan cheese

salt and pepper

To garnish:

deep-fried sage sprigs

Parmesan shavings

1 Heat half of the butter in a large saucepan and add the onion. Cook gently for 10 minutes until soft but not colored. Stir in the red chiles and cook for 1 minute. Add the pumpkin and cook, stirring constantly, for 5 minutes.

2 Stir in the rice to coat it with the butter and vegetables. Cook for 2 minutes to toast the grains. Add the stock, a large ladleful at a time, stirring until each ladleful is absorbed into the rice. Continue adding stock and cook until the rice is tender and creamy but the grains are still firm and the pumpkin is beginning to disintegrate. This should take about 20 minutes depending on the type of rice used. Taste and season well with salt and pepper then stir in the chopped sage, the remaining butter, and the Parmesan cheese.

3 Cover the pan and leave the risotto to rest for a few minutes, then serve garnished with deep-fried sage sprigs and Parmesan shavings.

Serves 6
Preparation time: 10 minutes
Cooking time: about 40 minutes

roasted vegetable pizza

2 cups bread flour

½ teaspoon salt

1 teaspoon quick-rising dry yeast

2½ tablespoons olive oil

¾ cup warm (110°F) water

Filling:

1 small pumpkin, about 1 pound

2 zucchini, thickly sliced

2 red onions, cut into thin wedges

2 red bell peppers, cored, seeded, and sliced

5 tablespoons olive oil

¾ cup sliced cremini mushrooms

1 cup halved cherry tomatoes

5 tablespoons sun-dried tomato paste

1½ cups thinly sliced mozzarella cheese

½ cup grated Parmesan cheese

salt and pepper

1 To make the pizza dough, put the flour, salt, and yeast into a bowl. Add the oil and warm water and mix to a dough, then knead on a lightly floured surface for 5–10 minutes until smooth and elastic. Put the dough into a lightly oiled bowl, cover with plastic wrap, and leave to rise while preparing the filling.

2 Scoop the seeds and fibers out of the pumpkin. Cut it into thin wedges and cut away the skin. Place the flesh in a roasting pan with the zucchini, onions, and peppers. Drizzle with the oil and a little salt and pepper and roast in a preheated oven at 425°F for 25 minutes until lightly colored. Stir in the mushrooms and cherry tomatoes and roast for a further 10 minutes.

3 Lightly grease and flour a large baking sheet. Roll out the pizza dough into a 12–13-inch round and place on the baking sheet. Spread with the tomato paste.

4 Arrange the roasted vegetables evenly over the pizza base. Scatter with the mozzarella, then the Parmesan and season with a little salt and pepper. Bake in a preheated oven at 425°F, for about 20 minutes, until the base is crisp and the cheese melted. Serve hot with a leafy salad.

Serves 3–4
Preparation time: 25 minutes, plus rising time
Cooking time: about 55 minutes

pasta triangles with pumpkin and sage

2 cups cubed pumpkin flesh

1 garlic clove, crushed

2 sage sprigs

3 tablespoons extra virgin olive oil

½ cup ricotta cheese

⅓ cup grated Parmesan cheese

salt and pepper

Pasta dough:

1 cup pasta flour, plus extra for dusting

1 teaspoon salt

1 egg, plus 1 small yolk

1 tablespoon extra virgin olive oil

2–3 tablespoons cold water

Sauce:

⅓ cup butter

2 tablespoons chopped sage

pepper

To garnish:

lemon wedges

Parmesan shavings

1 First make the pasta dough. Sift the flour and salt into a bowl, make a well in the middle and gradually work in the egg, egg yolk, oil, and enough water to make a soft dough. Turn out onto a lightly floured surface and knead gently for 5 minutes until the dough is smooth and elastic. Brush with a little oil, cover, and leave to rest for 30 minutes.

2 Place the pumpkin in a small roasting pan with the garlic, sage, oil, and salt and pepper. Cover loosely with foil and roast in a preheated oven at 400°F for 10 minutes, until soft. Transfer to a bowl, mash well, and set aside until cold.

3 Beat the ricotta and Parmesan into the pumpkin purèe and season with salt and pepper to taste.

4 Divide the pasta dough into four pieces and, using a pasta machine, roll out these pieces into long thin strips. Next, cut each strip into seven 3-inch squares (the size does not have to be exact as they can be trimmed after filling). Take spoonfuls of the filling and set them in the middle of each square. Dampen the edges and fold the squares diagonally in half, to form triangles. Trim the pasta to make the triangles neat and transfer to a floured kitchen towel (at this stage, the triangles may be frozen and can then be cooked straight from the freezer, just increase the cooking time to about 5 minutes).

5 To make the sauce, melt the butter with the sage and pepper until it just begins to turn a nutty brown color. Set aside and keep warm.

6 Meanwhile, bring a large saucepan of lightly salted water to a rolling boil. Add the pasta triangles, bring back to a boil and cook for 2–3 minutes. Serve the pasta bathed in the sage butter, with a squeeze of lemon juice and Parmesan shavings.

Serves 4
Preparation time: 20 minutes, plus resting time
Cooking time: about 20 minutes

root vegetable pasta with bacon

1 pumpkin or squash, about ¾ pound

½ pound small parsnips

10 ounces rutabagas or small turnips

3 tablespoons olive oil

1 onion, finely chopped

3 thin slices of lean bacon, chopped

1 garlic clove, crushed

1 x 16-ounce can chopped tomatoes

½ cup chicken or vegetable stock

1½ tablespoons clear honey (optional)

4 tablespoons chopped flat leaf parsley

7 ounces pasta (bowties, penne or shells)

grated Cheddar cheese, to serve

If you've never thought of combining pasta with root vegetables, you're in for a big surprise with this lovely, warming winter recipe. The sweet flavor of the parsnips and rutabagas is further enhanced with a little chopped bacon, a hint of garlic, and a large handful of parsley.

1 Cut the pumpkin or squash into wedges. Scoop out and discard the seeds and fibers and cut away the skin, then dice the flesh. Peel and dice the parsnips and rutabagas or turnips.

2 Heat the oil in a saucepan, add the onion and bacon and fry for about 3 minutes until lightly colored. Add the garlic, chopped tomatoes, stock, honey, if using, the prepared vegetables, and parsley. Bring to a boil, then reduce the heat, cover the pan, and simmer gently for about 15 minutes or until the vegetables are tender.

3 Meanwhile, cook the pasta in a large pan of boiling water for about 10 minutes until al dente—tender but firm to the bite.

4 Drain the pasta and add to the sauce. Toss together until well combined. Serve sprinkled with cheese, and accompanied by steamed spinach or broccoli.

Serves 2
Preparation time: 10–15 minutes
Cooking time: about 25 minutes

chickpea, spinach, and pumpkin stew with tomato aïoli

3 cups dried chickpeas

2 tablespoons olive oil

1 onion, finely chopped

1 garlic clove, finely chopped

4 cups peeled, diced pumpkin

2 cups chicken or vegetable stock

1 bay leaf

pinch of saffron threads

1 pound spinach, washed

1½ tablespoons cider or white wine vinegar

salt and pepper

Tomato aïoli:

1 fresh red chile, roasted, peeled, seeded, and chopped

4–6 garlic cloves, crushed

2 egg yolks

3–5 tablespoons fresh lemon juice

1 cup extra virgin olive oil

1½ tablespoons sun-dried tomato paste

1 Soak the chickpeas overnight. Drain the chickpeas, rinse well, and place in a large saucepan with about 4 cups of water to cover. Bring to a boil, then reduce the heat and simmer for 45 minutes–1 hour, or until tender. Drain and set aside.

2 Meanwhile, make the aïoli. Put the red chile on a baking sheet, place it under a preheated broiler and cook for 5–10 minutes until charred and blistered all over. Remove the chile from the heat, put it into a plastic bag, close securely, and leave to cool. When the chile is cool enough to handle, peel off the skin, remove the membranes and seeds, and roughly chop the flesh.

3 Place the garlic, egg yolks, and chile in a food processor, add 3 tablespoons of the lemon juice and process briefly to mix. With the motor running, gradually add the olive oil in a thin steady stream (as if making mayonnaise), until the mixture forms a thick cream. Scoop into a serving bowl and season to taste with salt and pepper and more lemon juice if required. Stir in the sun-dried tomato paste, and set aside.

4 Heat the oil in a large heatproof casserole over a moderate heat, add the onion and garlic and cook for 6–8 minutes until softened and lightly golden. Add the pumpkin, stock, bay leaf, saffron, and chickpeas. Season with salt and pepper and bring to a boil, then reduce the heat and simmer for 10–15 minutes until the pumpkin is tender.

5 Stir in the spinach, cover the pan, and cook, stirring occasionally, until the spinach just wilts. Stir in the vinegar and adjust the seasoning to taste. Serve in large individual bowls and pass around the aïoli, to stir into each serving.

Serves 4
Preparation time: 35 minutes, plus overnight soaking
Cooking time: 1–1½ hours

pumpkin and root vegetable stew

1 pumpkin, about 3 pounds

4 tablespoons sunflower or olive oil

1 large onion, finely chopped

3–4 garlic cloves, crushed

1 small red chile, seeded and chopped

4 celery sticks, cut into 1-inch lengths

2½ cups carrots, cut into 1-inch pieces

1¼ cups parsnips, cut into 1-inch pieces

2 x 16-ounce cans plum tomatoes

3 tablespoons tomato purée

1–2 tablespoons hot paprika

½–1 cup light vegetable stock

1 bouquet garni

2 x 15-ounce cans red kidney beans, drained

salt and pepper

3–4 tablespoons finely chopped parsley, to garnish

This rich stew is substantial and filling. Serve it with crusty bread or garlic mashed potatoes for a main course or supper dish. It will keep for 2–3 days in the refrigerator and improves with time, like most stews.

1 Slice the pumpkin in half across its widest part and discard the seeds and fibers. Cut the flesh into cubes, removing the skin. You should have about 2 pounds of flesh.

2 Heat the oil in a large saucepan and fry the onion, garlic, and chile until soft but not colored. Add the pumpkin and celery and fry gently for 10 minutes. Stir in the carrots, parsnips, tomatoes, tomato purèe, paprika, stock, and bouquet garni. Bring to a boil, then reduce the heat, cover the pan, and simmer for 1–1½ hours until the vegetables are almost tender.

3 Add the beans and cook for 10 minutes. To serve, season with salt and pepper and garnish with the parsley.

Serves 8–10
Preparation time: 20 minutes
Cooking time: 1¾–2 hours

pumpkin curry

1 tablespoon vegetable oil

1 onion, halved and thinly sliced

4 garlic cloves, crushed

1 teaspoon ground cumin

2 teaspoons ground coriander

1 fresh green chile, finely chopped

1¾ cups coconut milk

1 cup hot water

1 pumpkin, about 1½ pounds, cut into 2-inch cubes

2 tablespoons chopped cilantro leaves

sea salt and pepper

rice, to serve

1 Heat the oil in a large saucepan, add the onion and sauté until soft and lightly browned. Add the garlic, cumin, ground coriander, and chile, and sauté for 1 more minute.

2 Pour in the coconut milk, hot water, and pumpkin and bring to a boil. Lower the heat, cover the pan, and simmer gently for 10–15 minutes, or until the pumpkin is tender.

3 Season with salt and pepper and stir in the chopped cilantro. Serve hot, with rice.

Serves 4
Preparation time: 10 minutes
Cooking time: 15–20 minutes

baked pumpkin with mascarpone and sage

4 small pumpkins, each about 1 pound

6 tablespoons olive oil

1 cup chopped pancetta or smoked bacon

2 garlic cloves, crushed

½ cup thinly sliced sun-dried tomatoes

2 tablespoons chopped sage

½ cup mascarpone cheese

5 tablespoons grated Parmesan cheese

salt and pepper

To serve:

hot crusty bread

leafy salad

If you can only find larger pumpkins weighing about 1½–1¾ pounds, serve each person half a pumpkin, roasted and filled as in the recipe.

1 Cut a thin slice off the top of each pumpkin. Scoop out the seeds and fibers. Place the pumpkins in a roasting pan, putting the tops, flesh side up, next to the whole shells. Brush the inside of the pumpkins and the lids with 4 tablespoons of the oil and season with salt and plenty of black pepper. Bake in a preheated oven at 425°F for 20 minutes until softened and beginning to brown.

2 Meanwhile, heat the remaining oil and fry the pancetta or bacon until crisp and golden. Add the garlic, tomatoes, and sage and cook for 2 minutes.

3 Pile the mixture into the pumpkin shells. Spoon on the mascarpone and sprinkle with the Parmesan cheese. Return to the oven for a further 20 minutes. Serve hot with crusty bread and a leafy salad.

Serves 4
Preparation time: 15 minutes
Cooking time: 40 minutes

tea-smoked duck with roasted pumpkin salad

1 pumpkin, about 1 pound

3 tablespoons sunflower oil

½ teaspoon salt

1 teaspoon Thai seven-spice powder

⅔ cup jasmine tea leaves

½ cup rice

½ cup light brown sugar

2 star anise pods

2 small duck breasts, about 7 ounces each

3 ounces frisée lettuce

1 tablespoon chopped chives

Dressing:

1-inch piece fresh ginger root, peeled and grated

1 tablespoon rice vinegar

½ mild red chile, cored, seeded, and thinly sliced

4 tablespoons sunflower oil

½ teaspoon superfine sugar

salt and pepper

This unusual but delicious dish is adapted from a Chinese recipe.

1 Scoop out and discard the seeds and fibers from the pumpkin and cut it into thin wedges. Cut away the skin and place the wedges in a roasting pan. Drizzle with all but 1 teaspoon of the oil and season with salt and pepper to taste. Roast in a preheated oven at 425°F for 20 minutes, or until golden.

2 Meanwhile, brush the duck breasts with the reserved teaspoon of oil and rub with the salt and Thai seven-spice powder.

3 Line a wok with foil. Mix the tea, rice, sugar, and the star anise pods in the foil-lined wok and place a wire rack or trivet on top. Put the duck breasts on the rack, cover with a tight-fitting lid or foil and cook over a moderate heat for 15 minutes. Remove the wok from the heat and set aside, still covered, for 5 minutes.

4 Mix together all the dressing ingredients. Toss the frisée in a bowl with the dressing, chives, and roasted pumpkin then transfer to serving plates. Slice the duck breasts diagonally and arrange on the salad.

Serves 2
Preparation time: 20 minutes
Cooking time: 40 minutes

pumpkin and ginger ice cream

1 small pumpkin, about 1 pound

4 tablespoons lime juice

2 pieces crystallized ginger from a jar, finely chopped

4 egg yolks

⅔ cup light muscovado sugar

1 cup heavy cream

pumpkin seed caramel, to serve (see below)

1 Scoop out the seeds and fibers from the pumpkin. Slice it into wedges and cut away the skin. Cut the flesh into 1-inch pieces and steam over a pan of simmering water for 10–15 minutes until tender. Remove from the heat and leave to cool.

2 Blend the pumpkin in a food processor with the lime juice to make a smooth purèe. Add the ginger and blend briefly to combine.

3 Put the egg yolks and sugar in a bowl set over a pan of simmering water and whisk until thick and creamy. Stir in the pumpkin purée.

4 Whisk the cream in a separate bowl until it forms soft peaks. Using a large metal spoon, fold the cream into the pumpkin mixture until evenly combined. Put into a freezer container and freeze for several hours or overnight until firm.

5 Transfer the ice cream to the refrigerator about 45 minutes before serving to soften slightly. Serve scooped into bowls with the pumpkin seed caramel.

Serves 6
Preparation time: 15 minutes, plus cooling and freezing time
Cooking time: 10–15 minutes

pumpkin seed brittle

¼ cup water

¾ cup superfine sugar

2 tablespoons corn syrup

1¼ cups toasted pumpkin seeds

1 Pour the water into a heavy-based saucepan and add the sugar and corn syrup. Simmer gently until the sugar has dissolved and forms a light syrup.

2 Place the pumpkin seeds on a lightly oiled piece of foil. Pour the syrup over the seeds and allow to set for 1 hour.

3 Once the brittle has set, break into pieces, and serve with the ice cream.

Serves 6
Preparation time: 5 minutes, plus setting time
Cooking time: 5 minutes

pumpkin and rum mousse

4 tablespoons water

2 teaspoons powdered gelatin

1 pumpkin, about 2 pounds

finely grated zest and juice of 2 lemons

½ cup superfine sugar

4 tablespoons rum

2 egg whites

½ cup heavy cream

To decorate:

confectioners' sugar

mint sprigs

Use brandy or an orange-flavored liqueur if you don't like rum.

1 Put the water in a small bowl, sprinkle over the gelatin, and leave for at least 5 minutes. Discard the seeds and fibers from the pumpkin. Slice the pumpkin into wedges and cut away the skin. Cut the flesh into 1-inch pieces and steam over a pan of simmering water for 10–15 minutes until tender. Transfer to a food processor or blender, and purée the cooked flesh.

2 Put pumpkin purée into a saucepan with the lemon zest and juice and half the sugar and heat through for 1 minute. Press through a sieve into a bowl and stir in the gelatin until dissolved. Add the rum and allow to cool.

3 Whisk the egg whites until they form soft peaks. Gradually whisk in the remaining sugar until the mixture is stiff and glossy. Whip the cream until it forms soft peaks.

4 Using a large metal spoon, fold the cream, then the meringue, into the pumpkin mixture. Spoon into 6–8 tall serving glasses and chill for at least 1 hour until set. Serve dusted with confectioners' sugar and decorated with mint sprigs.

Serves 6–8
Preparation time: 15 minutes, plus chilling time
Cooking time: 10–15 minutes

steamed pumpkin pudding

1 pumpkin, about ¾ pound

1 cup self-rising flour

¼ cup unsalted butter, cut into small pieces

½ cup white breadcrumbs

½ cup light brown sugar

1½ cups raisins

2 eggs

1½ ounces fresh ginger root, finely chopped

lightly whipped and sweetened cream, to serve

This steamed pudding can also be cooked in individual ½-cup pudding molds. Put the molds in a roasting pan, half-fill the pan with very hot water and cover with foil. Bake in a preheated oven at 325°F for about 45 minutes.

1 Scoop out the seeds and fibers from the pumpkin and discard. Slice the pumpkin into wedges and cut away the skin. Coarsely grate the flesh.

2 Sift the flour into a bowl, add the butter, and rub in with fingertips. Add the breadcrumbs, sugar, and raisins.

3 Beat the eggs with the ginger and add to the bowl. Stir lightly until the ingredients are well mixed. Turn into a 5-cup pudding mold that's been buttered and lined with baking parchment. Cover with a double layer of parchment, securing the paper under the rim of the basin with string. Cover with foil, crumpling the edges of the foil under the string.

4 Put the pudding into a steamer over a pan of simmering water, or into a large saucepan and half-fill it with boiling water. Cover and steam for 2 hours, checking the water level occasionally.

5 To serve, loosen the edges of the pudding with a knife and invert it onto a warmed serving plate. Serve with the whipped cream.

Serves 6
Preparation time: 30 minutes
Cooking time: 2 hours

classic pumpkin pie

2 cups all-purpose flour

½ cup plus 2 tablespoons unsalted butter, cut into small pieces

3 tablespoons superfine sugar

1–2 tablespoons cold water

Filling:

1 pumpkin, about 1½ pounds

1 cup light cream

2 eggs

½ cup maple syrup

4 tablespoons all-purpose flour

1 teaspoon ground ginger

1 teaspoon ground cinnamon

lightly whipped and sweetened cream, to serve

If you have time, roll out the pastry trimmings and cut out maple leaves, or other simple leaf shapes. Bake them separately until golden and scatter around the edges of the pie after it is cooked.

1 To make the pastry, put the flour into a food processor or blender, add the butter, and process until the mixture resembles breadcrumbs. Add the sugar and cold water and blend to a dough, adding a drop more water if the mixture is too crumbly. (Alternatively, sift the flour into a mixing bowl, cut in the butter, then add the sugar and water and mix to a dough.) Wrap the dough in foil and chill for 30 minutes.

2 Scoop out the seeds and fibers from the pumpkin. Cut the pumpkin into large wedges and cook in a steamer over a pan of gently simmering water for 15–20 minutes until the flesh is tender. Scoop the flesh away from the skin with a spoon and put it into a food processor or blender. Blend until smooth then transfer to a bowl. Add the cream, eggs, maple syrup, flour, and spices and beat until evenly combined.

3 Roll out the pastry on a lightly floured surface and use to line a 9-inch tart pan with a removable bottom, or a deep pie plate.

4 Pour the pumpkin mixture into the pastry case and place it on a baking sheet. Bake in a preheated oven at 400°F for about 30 minutes, until the pastry is golden and the filling feels just firm to the touch. Serve warm with lightly whipped and sweetened cream.

Serves 6–8
Preparation time: 30 minutes, plus chilling time
Cooking time: 50 minutes

pumpkin and almond tart

1½ cups all-purpose flour

6 tablespoons unsalted butter, cut into pieces

2 tablespoons superfine sugar

1 teaspoon cold water

lightly whipped and sweetened cream, to serve

Filling:

½ small pumpkin, about 1 pound

½ cup unsalted butter

½ cup superfine sugar

2 eggs

¾ cup ground almonds

½ teaspoon almond extract

To glaze:

5 tablespoons apricot jam

2 tablespoons water

1 To make the pastry, put the flour into a food processor with the butter and blend until the mixture resembles breadcrumbs. Add the sugar and cold water and mix into a dough, adding a little more water if the mixture is too crumbly. (Alternatively, sift the flour into a mixing bowl, cut in the butter, then add the sugar and water.) Wrap the pastry in plastic wrap and chill for 30 minutes.

2 Scoop out the seeds and fibers from the pumpkin and cut away the skin. Cut the flesh into ¾-inch pieces. Melt 2 tablespoons of the butter in a frying pan, add 3 tablespoons of the sugar and heat gently until the sugar dissolves. Add the pumpkin pieces and cook gently for about 5 minutes until the sugar caramelizes. Allow to cool slightly.

3 Roll out the pastry on a lightly floured surface and use to line an 8-inch tart pan with a removable bottom.

4 Beat the remaining butter and sugar into a paste. Add the eggs, almonds, and almond extract and beat well. Spread the mixture over the pastry base and scatter with the pumpkin pieces.

5 Bake the tart in a preheated oven at 375°F for about 30 minutes, until the almond mixture rises around the pumpkin pieces and is a pale golden color. Melt the apricot jam in a saucepan with the water and press through a sieve. Brush over the tart and serve warm or cold with the whipped cream, if wished.

Serves 6–8
Preparation time: 20 minutes, plus chilling time
Cooking time: about 45 minutes

pumpkin and almond pithiviers

1 pumpkin, about 1 pound

finely grated zest and juice of 2 lemons

½ cup superfine sugar

½ teaspoon cornstarch

1½ tablespoons water

5 tablespoons orange-flavored liqueur or orange juice

½ cup unsalted butter, softened

1 egg

2 cups ground almonds

1 pound puff pastry

beaten egg, to glaze

confectioners' sugar, for dusting

lightly whipped and sweetened cream (optional), to serve

1 Scoop out the seeds and fibers from the pumpkin. Slice the pumpkin into wedges and cut away the skin. Cut the flesh into ½-inch dice and put them in a saucepan with the lemon juice and 4 tablespoons of the sugar. Mix the cornstarch with the water and add to the pan. Cook, stirring, until the pumpkin is coated in glossy juices. Remove the pan from the heat, add the liqueur or orange juice and allow to cool.

2 Beat the butter in a bowl with the remaining sugar, egg, ground almonds, and lemon zest to make a paste.

3 Lightly grease a baking sheet and sprinkle with water. Roll out half the puff pastry on a lightly floured surface and cut out a 10-inch circle. Transfer it to the baking sheet. Spread the pumpkin mixture to within 1-inch of the edge. Spoon the almond mixture over the pumpkin.

4 Roll out the remaining pastry to a 10½-inch circle. Brush the edges of the pastry base with beaten egg and place the pastry lid over the filling, pressing it firmly around the edges to seal. Flute the edges of the pie to decorate.

5 Brush the pie with beaten egg to glaze; using the tip of a sharp knife, mark faint lines radiating out from the center to the edges. Bake the pie in a preheated oven at 425°F for 25–30 minutes, until it is well-risen and golden. Remove from the oven and increase the temperature to 450°F. Dust the pastry lid very generously with confectioners' sugar and return the pie to the oven for a further 3–4 minutes, watching closely, until the sugar caramelizes to a glossy glaze. Serve warm or cold with cream, if wished.

Serves 8
Preparation time: 25 minutes
Cooking time: about 35 minutes

pumpkin and raisin cheesecake

1 cup raisins

3 tablespoons orange-flavored liqueur

6 ounces gingersnap cookies

¼ cup unsalted butter, melted

1 pumpkin, about 14 ounces

1 pound cottage cheese

2 eggs

½ cup heavy cream

⅓ cup superfine sugar

finely grated zest and juice of ½ an orange

To serve:

lightly whipped and sweetened cream

caramelized orange zest slivers

1 Put the raisins into a small bowl with the liqueur and leave to soak for 15 minutes. Meanwhile, lightly oil the sides of an 8-inch springform pan. Put the cookies into a zip-top freezer bag and crush them with a rolling pin. Transfer to a bowl and add the melted butter. Stir until evenly mixed. Turn the mixture into the pan and pack down onto the base and slightly up the sides.

2 Scoop out the seeds and fibers from the pumpkin, then cut it into large wedges. Put the wedges in a steamer over a pan of gently simmering water and cook for 15–20 minutes until the flesh is tender. Remove from the heat and allow to cool.

3 Put the cottage cheese in a food processor and blend for about 1 minute until completely smooth. Scoop the pumpkin flesh into the processor and blend until smooth. Add the eggs, cream, sugar, and orange zest and juice and blend briefly until smooth.

4 Scatter the raisins over the cookie base, stirring any remaining liqueur into the cottage cheese mixture. Ladle the mixture over the base.

5 Bake the cheesecake in a preheated oven at 350°F for 40 minutes, until the center feels just firm to the touch. Leave it to cool in the pan, then chill until you are ready to serve. Serve with lightly whipped and sweetened cream topped with caramelized orange zest slivers.

Serves 6–8
Preparation time: 20 minutes, plus cooling and chilling time
Cooking time: about 1 hour

pumpkin crème brûlées

½ small pumpkin, about ½ pound

3 passion fruits

4 egg yolks

½ cup superfine sugar

2 cups heavy cream

1 teaspoon vanilla extract

1 Scoop out the seeds and fibers from the pumpkin. Slice the pumpkin into wedges and cut away the skin. Cut the flesh into ½-inch dice and divide among six ¾-cup ramekins. Halve the passion fruits and scoop the pulp over the pumpkin.

2 Put the egg yolks and half the sugar into a bowl and whisk lightly. Warm the cream and vanilla extract in a heavy-based saucepan until just hand-hot. Pour over the egg mixture, whisking until combined.

3 Strain the mixture through a sieve into a jug, then pour the mixture into the ramekins. Stand the dishes in a roasting pan and pour in ½-inch hot water. Bake in a preheated oven at 350°F for about 25 minutes, until very lightly set. Remove the ramekins from the pan and leave to cool. Cover and chill for several hours or overnight.

4 Sprinkle the tops of the brûlées with the remaining sugar and put them under the broiler for a few minutes, watching them closely until the sugar caramelizes. Leave to cool, then chill until ready to serve.

Serves 6
Preparation time: 25 minutes, plus cooling and chilling time
Cooking time: about 35 minutes

pumpkin blondies

1 pumpkin, about 1 pound

10 ounces white chocolate, broken into pieces

1 cup unsalted butter

1 cup cream cheese

⅔ cup superfine sugar

3 eggs

¾ cup all-purpose flour

1 teaspoon vanilla extract

3 tablespoons pumpkin seeds

1 Line a shallow 11 x 7-inch rectangular pan with baking parchment. Scoop out the seeds and fibers from the pumpkin. Cut away the skin and cut the flesh into ½-inch dice.

2 Put the chocolate into a heatproof bowl with the butter and melt over a pan of gently simmering water. Stir until smooth.

3 Whisk the cream cheese and chocolate butter mixture in a large bowl until softened. Gradually whisk in the sugar, then the eggs, flour, and vanilla extract until the mixture is smooth. Pour half the mixture into the pan and scatter with half the chopped pumpkin. Spoon over the remaining egg mixture, then scatter with the remaining pumpkin pieces and the pumpkin seeds.

4 Bake the blondies in a preheated oven at 375°F for 25 minutes until the surface feels just firm but still wobbly underneath. Allow to cool in the pan. Cut into squares before serving.

Makes 15 squares
Preparation time: 15 minutes, plus cooling time
Cooking time: 25 minutes

pumpkin bars

½ small pumpkin, about ½ pound

1 cup self-rising flour

1 cup unsweetened coconut flakes

1½ cups rolled oats or quick-cooking rolled oats

½ cup unsalted butter

½ cup superfine sugar

3 tablespoons clear honey

Scotch oats or Irish oatmeal can be used instead of the rolled oats and coconut to produce a bar that is more like a granola bar in appearance and flavor.

1 Scoop out the seeds and fibers from the pumpkin. Slice the pumpkin into wedges and cut away the skin. Coarsely grate the flesh.

2 In a bowl, mix together the flour, coconut, oats, and grated pumpkin. Melt the butter in a small saucepan with the sugar and honey and add to the bowl. Mix until evenly combined.

3 Turn the mixture into a lightly greased 9-inch square cake pan and spread into the corners. Bake in a preheated oven at 350°F for 25 minutes until slightly risen and a pale golden color.

4 Allow the cake to cool in the pan, then cut into bars and transfer to an airtight container. The bars can be stored in a cool place for 4–5 days.

Makes 12 bars
Preparation time: 15 minutes
Cooking time: 25 minutes

pumpkin halloween cookies

½ small pumpkin, about ½ pound

3 cups all-purpose flour

1 teaspoon ground ginger

½ teaspoon grated nutmeg

¾ cup plus 2 tablespoons unsalted butter, cut into small pieces

¾ cup confectioners' sugar

2 egg yolks

colored royal icing, to decorate

1 Scoop out and discard the seeds and fibers from the pumpkin. Slice the flesh into wedges and cut away the skin. Finely grate the flesh.

2 Put the flour, ginger, and nutmeg into a food processor. Add the butter and blend until the mixture resembles fine breadcrumbs. Add the grated pumpkin and confectioners' sugar and blend briefly until combined. Add the egg yolks and blend to form a soft dough. (Alternatively, put the flour in a mixing bowl and cut in the butter, then add the remaining ingredients and mix into a dough.) Wrap the dough in plastic wrap and chill for at least 2 hours, or overnight, until firm.

3 Lightly grease two baking sheets. Roll out the dough on a lightly floured surface and cut out pumpkin shapes with a cutter. Transfer the shapes to the baking sheets and re-roll the trimmings to make more cookies. Bake in a preheated oven at 350°F for 15–20 minutes, until golden. Allow to cool for 2 minutes then transfer to a wire rack to cool completely.

4 Decorate the cookies with different colored royal icing. Spoon some colored icing into a piping bag with a writing nozzle. Pipe around the edges of the cookies. Once this has dried, fill in with the same colored icing using a larger nozzle on the piping bag and smooth this out for total coverage. Allow this to dry, then decorate the cookies with patterns of your choice using the writing nozzle and different colored icing. Allow the icing to set for 1 hour before serving. Alternatively pipe your icing decoration straight on to the cookes and allow to dry. The cookies can be stored in an airtight container in a cool place for up to 2 days.

Makes about 12
Preparation time: 25 minutes, plus chilling and decorating time
Cooking time: 15–20 minutes

pumpkin and apple muffins

½ small pumpkin, about 1 pound

3 cups all-purpose flour

1 tablespoon and ½ teaspoon baking powder

1 teaspoon allspice

pinch of salt

1 tart apple (such as a Granny Smith), peeled, cored, and finely diced

⅔ cup superfine sugar

2 eggs

¾ cup milk

5 tablespoons pumpkin or vegetable oil

Muffins don't keep very well and are best eaten on the day they're baked, preferably slightly warm from the oven. If you want to make a batch in advance, freeze them in a container, packed individually, so they can be thawed as needed.

1 Line a 12-cup muffin pan with paper baking cups. Scoop out the seeds and fibers from the pumpkin. Slice the flesh into wedges and cut away the skin. Cut the flesh into ¼-inch dice.

2 Sift the flour, baking powder, allspice, and salt into a bowl and stir in the diced pumpkin, apple, and sugar. Beat together the eggs, milk, and oil, and add to the bowl. Using a large metal spoon, gently stir the ingredients together just until combined. Spoon into the muffin pan.

3 Bake the muffins in a preheated oven at 375°F for about 20–25 minutes, until well risen and a pale golden color. Transfer to a wire rack to cool. Serve warm or cold, lightly buttered if desired.

Makes 12 muffins
Preparation time: 15 minutes
Cooking time: 20–25 minutes

spicy pumpkin fruitcake

½ small pumpkin, about 1 pound

½ cup unsalted butter, softened

⅔ cup light brown sugar

2 eggs, lightly beaten

2 cups self-rising flour

1 tablespoon allspice (or 1½ teaspoons cinnamon and 1½ teaspoons nutmeg)

¾ cup golden raisins

¾ cup chopped dried apricots or peaches

¾ cup mixed chopped nuts

1½ tablespoons milk

2 tablespoons raw sugar, for sprinkling over the top

This deliciously moist cake improves in flavor and texture if it is kept for a day before cutting.

1 Grease and line an 8-inch round cake pan with baking parchment. Scoop out the seeds and fibers from the pumpkin. Slice the pumpkin into wedges and cut away the skin. Cut the flesh into ¼-inch dice.

2 Beat the butter and sugar until pale and creamy. Gradually beat in the eggs, a little at a time, adding a little of the flour to keep the mixture from curdling. Sift the flour and allspice into the bowl and stir them in.

3 Add the chopped pumpkin, dried fruits, nuts, and milk, and mix just until combined. Put the mixture in the prepared pan and level the surface. Sprinkle with the raw sugar. Bake in a preheated oven at 325°F for 1–1½ hours, until a skewer inserted into the center of the cake comes out clean.

4 Let the cake cool in the pan, then wrap, and store in a cool place for 4–5 days.

Makes one 8-inch cake
Preparation time: 15 minutes
Cooking time: 1–1½ hours

pumpkin pecan buns

1 pumpkin, about 1 pound

5 cups bread flour

½ teaspoon salt

1 teaspoon allspice (or ½ teaspoon cinnamon and ½ teaspoon nutmeg)

½ cup unsalted butter, cut into small pieces

⅓ cup plus 3 tablespoons superfine sugar

1 tablespoon quick-rising dry yeast

⅓ cup milk

1 teaspoon vanilla extract

1 egg

1 cup chopped pecans

¾ cup golden raisins

maple syrup, to glaze

1 Scoop out the seeds and fibers from the pumpkin. Slice the flesh into wedges and steam over a pan of simmering water for 15–20 minutes until the pumpkin is tender.

2 Meanwhile, put the flour, salt, and allspice into a bowl. Add the butter and rub in with the fingertips. Stir in the ⅓ cup sugar and the yeast.

3 Scoop the pumpkin flesh from the skin and mash the flesh in a bowl. Mix with the milk and vanilla extract. (The mashed pumpkin should make the milk hand hot. If it doesn't, heat through in a microwave or a small saucepan.) Add to the flour mixture with the egg and mix into a dough. Knead by hand or with an electric mixer for 5–10 minutes until smooth and elastic. Transfer to a lightly oiled bowl, cover with plastic wrap and leave in a warm place until doubled in size.

4 Grease an 11 x 7-inch baking pan. Turn out the dough onto a lightly floured surface and knead lightly to eliminate most of the air. Roll out into a 12-inch square. Sprinkle with the remaining sugar to within ¾-inch of the edges. Scatter with the pecans and raisins, then roll up the dough like a jelly roll.

5 Cut the roll into 12 slices and arrange them, cut sides up, in the prepared pan. Cover with oiled plastic wrap and leave to rise until the dough has doubled in size and is rising over the sides of the pan, about 30–45 minutes. Bake in a preheated oven at 400°F for about 30 minutes, until a deep golden color. Transfer to a wire rack and brush with maple syrup to glaze. Break the bread into buns after it cools.

Makes 12 buns
Preparation time: 35 minutes, plus rising time
Cooking time: 45–50 minutes

sweet pumpkin and walnut bread

½ small pumpkin, about ½ pound

7½ cups bread flour

pinch of salt

¼ cup butter, cut into small pieces

1 tablespoon quick-rising dry yeast

5 tablespoons light brown sugar

1 cup walnut pieces, lightly toasted

4 tablespoons molasses

1 cup warm water

beaten egg or milk, to glaze

This bread freezes well and can be frozen for up to 3 months. Wrap the loaves in foil once they are completely cool.

1 Scoop out the seeds and fibers from the pumpkin. Slice the pumpkin into wedges and coarsely grate the flesh.

2 Put the flour and salt into a bowl with the butter and cut in using your fingertips. Stir in the yeast, sugar, walnut pieces, and grated pumpkin until evenly combined.

3 Mix the molasses with the warm water and add to the bowl. Mix into a soft dough, adding more water if the mixture is too dry. Knead for 10 minutes, either by hand or using the dough hook attachment of an electric mixer. Put the dough into a lightly oiled bowl, cover with plastic wrap and leave in a warm place for about 1 hour until the dough doubles in size.

4 Grease a 2-pound loaf pan and a 1-pound loaf pan. Turn out the dough onto a work surface and knead lightly to reduce the bulk. Place a third of the dough in the small pan and two-thirds in the large pan and leave in a warm place, lightly covered with oiled plastic wrap, until the dough rises above the rim of the pans.

5 Brush the dough with beaten egg or milk to glaze. Bake in a preheated oven at 425°F for 25 minutes for the small loaf and 35–40 minutes for the large loaf, until they are well risen and a deep golden color. Turn the loaves out of the pans and return them to the oven, on a baking sheet, for a few minutes or until the bases sounds hollow when lightly tapped. Allow to cool on a wire rack. Wrap the loaves in foil and store in an airtight container.

Makes one 2-pound loaf and one 1-pound loaf
Preparation time: 15 minutes, plus rising time
Cooking time: about 40 minutes

pumpkin scones

⅓ small pumpkin, about 6 ounces

2 cups self-rising flour

pinch of salt

1 teaspoon baking powder

¼ cup unsalted butter, cut into small pieces

3 tablespoons superfine sugar

½ cup chopped crystallized ginger

⅓–½ cup milk

beaten egg or milk, to glaze

To make deep, light-as-air scones, do not overhandle the dough and roll it out very thickly. Re-roll the trimmings to make extra scones.

1 Scoop out the seeds and fibers from the pumpkin. Slice the pumpkin into wedges and cut away the skin. Finely grate the flesh.

2 Put the flour, salt, and baking powder into a food processor with the butter and blend until the mixture resembles fine breadcrumbs. Add the sugar, ginger, and pumpkin and blend briefly to mix.

3 Blend in enough milk to make a fairly soft but not sticky dough. (Alternatively, put the flour into a bowl and cut in the butter, then add the remaining ingredients and mix into a dough.)

4 Grease a baking sheet. Roll out the dough on a floured surface to a ¾-inch thickness and cut into rounds with a 2–2½-inch cutter. Transfer the scones to the baking sheet and brush with beaten egg or milk to glaze.

5 Bake the scones in a preheated oven at 425°F for about 10 minutes, until risen and golden. Transfer to a wire rack to cool. Serve with butter and Pumpkin and Apple Jam (see page 63), if liked.

Makes 10 scones
Preparation time: 15 minutes
Cooking time: 10 minutes

pumpkin and orange marmalade

2 pounds oranges

juice of 2 lemons

12 cups water

1 pumpkin, about 1½ pounds

5 pounds granulated sugar

To sterilize jam jars, wash them thoroughly in hot soapy water and remove any labels, and any rubber seals from the jars. Put the jars into a preheated oven at 300°F for 15–20 minutes while boiling the jam and fill them while they are still hot.

1 Scrub the oranges, then cut them in half and squeeze out the juice, reserving the pith and seeds. Tie the pith and pips in a cheesecloth bag. Slice the orange peel into small pieces and put it into a preserving pan or a heavy-based saucepan with the orange juice, lemon juice, the cheesecloth bag, and the water. Simmer gently for about 1½–2 hours until the peel is very tender and the liquid has reduced.

2 Meanwhile, scoop out the seeds and fibers from the pumpkin. Slice the pumpkin into wedges and cut away the skin. Cut the flesh into ½-inch dice.

3 Remove the cheesecloth bag from the pan, squeezing it against the side of the pan to extract the juices. Add the pumpkin pieces and sugar and heat gently until the sugar has dissolved. Bring to a boil and boil until setting point has been reached, about 20–25 minutes. To test for a set, spoon a little marmalade onto a cold saucer and chill for 1 minute. Push the cooled syrup with a finger. If it wrinkles, it has reached the setting point.

4 Ladle the marmalade into sterilized jars and cover with lids or jam jar covers. The marmalade can be stored in a cool place for up to 6 months.

Makes about 4 pounds
Preparation time: about 45 minutes
Cooking time: about 2–2½ hours

caramelized pumpkin seeds

2 ounces pumpkin seeds

2 tablespoons confectioners' sugar

pinch of salt

½ teaspoon ground nutmeg

1 teaspoon ground cinnamon

½ teaspoon ground ginger

1 Put the pumpkin seeds and any of the fiber that clings to them in a bowl and cover with plenty of water. With your hands, squeeze the pulp so that the seeds rise to the surface, then rinse them through a strainer and drain on paper towels. Transfer the seeds to a baking sheet and shake it so that the seeds form a single layer. Bake in a preheated oven at 300°F for 30 minutes, then allow to cool.

2 When the pumpkin seeds are cool, put them in a heavy-based skillet with the sugar, salt, and all the spices and cook over a low heat for 2–3 minutes until they are coated in the spices.

3 Transfer the pumpkin seeds onto a plate, adding all the remaining sugar and spices in the pan, and leave to cool for 10 minutes. Use a fork to break up the seeds if they have stuck together. Transfer the seeds to an airtight container, where they will keep for up to 1 week.

Makes 2 ounces
Preparation time: 10 minutes, plus soaking and cooling time
Cooking time: about 35 minutes

spiced pumpkin seeds

½ teaspoon coriander seeds

½ teaspoon cumin seeds

2 ounces roasted pumpkin seeds

½ teaspoon superfine sugar

½ teaspoon salt

½ teaspoon ground turmeric

½ teaspoon celery salt

½ teaspoon cayenne pepper

1 teaspoon black onion seeds

1 Put the coriander and cumin seeds in a mortar and pound with a pestle until lightly crushed. Heat the oil in a heavy-based skillet. Add the pumpkin seeds, the sugar, salt, and all the spices and cook gently, stirring, for 2–3 minutes until the seeds begin to color.

2 Transfer the pumpkin seeds to a small bowl and allow to cool, then serve.

Makes 2 ounces
Preparation time: 5 minutes
Cooking time: 2–3 minutes

pumpkin and apple jam *(pictured on page 60)*

1 pumpkin, about 2 pounds

2 pounds granulated sugar

2 pounds cooking apples, peeled, cored, and roughly sliced

juice of 2 oranges

finely grated zest and juice of 3 lemons

1 Scoop out the seeds and fibers from the pumpkin. Slice the pumpkin into wedges and cut away the skin. Thinly slice the flesh and put it into a bowl with half the sugar. Cover and leave to stand overnight. (Most of the sugar will dissolve and turn syrupy as it stands.)

2 Put the pumpkin, the remaining sugar, and the sugary juices into a preserving pan or a large, heavy-based saucepan. Add the apples, orange juice, lemon zest and juice. Heat gently until the sugar dissolves.

3 Bring the mixture to a boil and cook until it reaches setting point, about 15–20 minutes. Test by spooning a little jam onto a saucer and chilling for 1 minute. Push the syrup; if it wrinkles, it has reached setting point. Ladle the jam into sterilized jars and cover with lids. The jam can be stored in a cool place for up to 6 months.

Makes about 4 pounds
Preparation time: 25 minutes, plus standing overnight
Cooking time: about 20 minutes

index

a
aïoli, tomato 27
almonds: pumpkin and almond pithiviers 44
pumpkin and almond tart 42
apples: pumpkin and apple jam 63
pumpkin and apple muffins 54

b
bacon: baked pumpkin with mascarpone and sage 32
root vegetable pasta with bacon 26
blondies, pumpkin 50
bread, sweet pumpkin and walnut 58

c
cakes: pumpkin bars 51
pumpkin blondies 50
pumpkin pecan buns 57
spicy pumpkin fruitcake 56
caramelized pumpkin seeds 62
carving pumpkins 8–10
cheese: baked pumpkin with mascarpone and sage 32
grilled pumpkin with Parmesan 16
pumpkin soup with crusty cheese topping 14
roasted vegetable pizza 22
cheesecake, pumpkin and raisin 46
chickpea, spinach and pumpkin stew 27
chocolate: pumpkin blondies 50
classic pumpkin pie 40
cookies, pumpkin Halloween 52
couscous and pumpkin pilaf 19
crème brûlées, pumpkin 48
crisps, pumpkin 12
curries: curried pumpkin and sweet onions 15
pumpkin curry 30

d
duck: tea-smoked duck with roasted pumpkin salad 34

f
fruitcake, spicy pumpkin 56

g
ginger: pumpkin and ginger ice cream 36
grilled pumpkin with Parmesan 16
growing pumpkins 6–8

h
Halloween 8

i
ice cream, pumpkin and ginger 36

j
jack-o-lanterns 8–10
jam, pumpkin and apple 63

m
marmalade, pumpkin and orange 61
mousse, pumpkin and rum 38
muffins, pumpkin and apple 54

o
oats, pumpkin bars 51
onions: curried pumpkin and sweet onions 15
oranges: pumpkin and orange marmalade 61

p
pasta: pasta triangles with pumpkin and sage 24
root vegetable pasta with bacon 26
pecan buns, pumpkin 57
peppers: roasted vegetable pizza 22
pies: classic pumpkin pie 40
pumpkin and almond pithiviers 44
pilaf, pumpkin and couscous 19
pine nut, pumpkin and oregano salad 18
pizza, roasted vegetable 22
pumpkin seeds 10
caramelized pumpkin seeds 62
pumpkin seed brittle 36
spiced pumpkin seeds 63

r
risotto, pumpkin, sage and chile 20
roasted pumpkin wedges 16
root vegetable pasta with bacon 26

s
salads: pumpkin, pine nut and oregano salad 18
tea-smoked duck with roasted pumpkin salad 34
scones, pumpkin 60
soups: pumpkin soup with crusty cheese topping 14
Tuscan pumpkin soup 12
spiced pumpkin seeds 63
spinach, chickpea and pumpkin stew 27
steamed pumpkin pudding 39
sweet pumpkin and walnut bread 58

t
tart, pumpkin and almond 42
tea-smoked duck with roasted pumpkin salad 34
Thanksgiving 10
tomato aïoli 27
Tuscan pumpkin soup 12

v
vegetables: pumpkin and root vegetable stew 28
root vegetable pasta with bacon 26

w
walnuts: sweet pumpkin and walnut bread 58

z
zucchini: pumpkin, pine nut and oregano salad 18
roasted vegetable pizza 22

Acknowledgments in Source Order
Octopus Publishing Group Limited/Graham Kirk 41, 53 /**Philip Webb** 2–3, 4–5, 7, 9, 10, 11, 12, 13, 17, 21, 23, 25, 29, 30, 31, 33, 35, 37, 42, 45, 47, 49, 50, 55, 59, 60, 62